Who Is the Holy Spirit?

Barbara H. Knuckles &
Ruth E. Van Reken

FISHERMAN
BIBLE STUDY SERIES

Who Is the Holy Spirit?

Published by WaterBrook Press

12265 Oracle Boulevard, Suite 200

Colorado Springs, CO 80921

Unless otherwise indicated, all Scripture quotations are taken from the Holy Bible: New International Version®. NIV®. Copyright © 1973, 1978, 1984 by International Bible Society. Used by permission of Zondervan Publishing House. All rights reserved. Scripture quotations marked (KJV) are taken from the King James Version.

ISBN 978-0-87788-853-6

Published in the United States by WaterBrook Multnomah, an imprint of the Crown Publishing Group, a division of Random House Inc., New York.

Printed in the United States of America

2013

20 19 18 17 16 15 14

Contents

How to Use This Studyguide

F isherman studyguides are based on the inductive approach to Bible study. Inductive study is discovery study; we discover what the Bible says as we ask questions about its content and search for answers. This is quite different from the process in which a teacher *tells* a group *about* the Bible—what it means and what to do about it. In inductive study, God speaks directly to each of us through his Word.

A group functions best when a leader keeps the discussion on target, but the leader is neither the teacher nor the "answer person." A leader's responsibility is to *ask*—not *tell*. The answers come from the text itself as group members examine, discuss, and think together about the passage.

There are four kinds of questions in each study. The first is an *approach question.* Asked and answered before the Bible passage is read, this question breaks the ice and helps you start thinking about the topic of the Bible study. It begins to reveal where thoughts and feelings need to be transformed by Scripture.

Some of the earlier questions in each study are *observation questions*—who, what, where, when, and how—designed to help you learn some basic facts about the passage of Scripture.

Once you know what the Bible says, you need to ask, *What does it mean?* These *interpretation questions* help you discover the writer's basic message.

Next come *application questions,* which ask, *What does it mean to me?* They challenge you to live out the Scripture's life-transforming message.

Fisherman studyguides provide spaces between questions for jotting down responses as well as any related questions you would like to raise in the group. Each group member should have a copy of the studyguide and may take a turn in leading the group.

A group should use any accurate, modern translation of the Bible such as the *New International Version,* the *New American Standard Bible,* the *New Living Translation,* the *New Revised Standard Version,* the *New Jerusalem Bible,* or the *Good News Bible.* (Other translations or paraphrases of the Bible may be referred to when additional help is needed.) Bible commentaries should not be brought to a Bible study because they tend to dampen discussion and keep people from thinking for themselves.

Suggestions for Group Leaders

1. Thoroughly read and study the Bible passage before the meeting. Get a firm grasp on its themes and begin applying its teachings for yourself. Pray that the Holy Spirit will "guide you into all truth" (John 16:13) so that your leadership will guide others.

2. If any of the studyguide's questions seem ambiguous or unnatural to you, rephrase them, feeling free to add others that seem necessary to bring out the meaning of a verse.

3. Begin (and end) the study promptly. Start by asking someone to pray that every participant will both understand the passage and be open to its transforming power. Remember, the Holy Spirit is the teacher, not you!

4. Ask for volunteers to read the passages aloud.

5. As you ask the studyguide's questions in sequence, encourage everyone to participate in the discussion. If some are silent, try gently suggesting, "Let's have an answer from someone who hasn't spoken up yet."

6. If a question comes up that you can't answer, don't be afraid to admit that you're baffled. Assign the topic as a research project for someone to report on next week, or say, "I'll do some studying and let you know what I find out."

7. Keep the discussion moving, but be sure it stays focused. Though a certain number of tangents are inevitable, you'll want to quickly bring the discussion back to the topic at hand. Also, learn to pace the discussion so that you finish the lesson in the time allotted.

8. Don't be afraid of silences; some questions take time to answer, and some people need time to gather courage to speak. If silence persists, rephrase your question, but resist the temptation to answer it yourself.

9. If someone comes up with an answer that is clearly illogical or unbiblical, ask for further clarification: "What verse suggests that to you?"

10. Discourage overuse of cross references. Learn all you can from the passage at hand, while selectively incorporating a few important references suggested in the studyguide.

11. Some questions are marked with a ✎. This indicates that further information is available in the Leader's Notes at the back of the guide.

12. For more information on getting a new Bible study group started and keeping it functioning effectively, read *You Can Start a Bible Study Group* by Gladys M. Hunt and *Pilgrims in Progress: Growing Through Groups* by Jim and Carol Plueddemann. (Both books are available from WaterBrook Press.)

Suggestions for Group Members

1. Learn and apply the following ground rules for effective Bible study. (If new members join the group later, review these guidelines with the whole group.)

2. Remember that your goal is to learn all you can *from the Bible passage being studied.* Let it speak for itself without using Bible commentaries or other Bible passages. There is more than enough in each assigned passage to keep your group productively occupied for one session. Sticking to the passage saves the group from insecurity ("I don't have the right reference books—or the time to read anything else.") and confusion ("Where did *that* come from? I thought we were studying _____.").

3. Avoid the temptation to bring up those fascinating tangents that don't really grow out of the passage you are discussing. If the topic is of common interest, you can bring it up later in informal conversation after the study. Meanwhile, help one another stick to the subject.

4. Encourage one another to participate. People remember best what they discover and verbalize for

themselves. Some people are naturally shy, while others may be afraid of making a mistake. If your discussion is free and friendly and you show real interest in what other group members think and feel, the quieter ones will be more likely to speak up. Remember, the more people involved in a discussion, the richer it will be.

5. Guard yourself from answering too many questions or talking too much. Give others a chance to share their ideas. If you are one who participates easily, discipline yourself by counting to ten before you open your mouth.

6. Make personal, honest applications and commit yourself to letting God's Word change you.

Introduction

Christians worship one God who is three distinct persons in his being. This is the mystery of the Trinity. *God the Father* is revealed in the Bible through his creation, his acts in history, and through metaphors and prophecies. *Jesus Christ, the Son of God,* is described in the New Testament gospels as a historical person who was seen, heard, and touched by his disciples. We can grasp some of who he is and picture what he might have been like. But *God the Holy Spirit,* the third person of the Trinity, is far more elusive.

How can we know what the Holy Spirit is like? John 3:8 likens the Holy Spirit to the wind: "The wind blows wherever it pleases. You hear its sound, but you cannot tell where it comes from or where it is going. So it is with everyone born of the Spirit." This is an appropriate analogy, since the words used in the Bible for *spirit* (Greek *pneuma* and Hebrew *ruah*) mean "wind," "breath," or "divine power." It's hard to pin down the wind, but that doesn't make it any less real or powerful. Just like the Spirit, the wind's influence and effect is felt, even though it is invisible.

If you think of the following studies as colorful kites dancing on the breath of God, revealing his currents of love and power, you will get a growing sense of what the Holy Spirit is like. As you see how God's Spirit moves and works, he will become personal and real rather than some vague force.

Though no lesson in this studyguide is exhaustive or even comprehensive, in each one you will find insights from God's Word that may cause you to shout "Glory!" or that may whisper peace and comfort to you. For by means of the Holy Spirit, sin's aftermath of alienation from God is exchanged for new connections: with God our Father; with each other; with ourselves; and with purpose, truth, grace, and life. Through Christ's death on the cross we have forgiveness and redemption. Through the Spirit we are able to live as children of God, in power and wisdom and unity, equipped for every good work.

The Spirit
of Truth

JOHN 14:15-27; 15:26-27; 16:5-15

There are three large cardboard boxes in my living room, all draped with old blankets. Cut into each box are various peepholes, doors, and hatches. One morning these boxes became either submarines or houses—depending on which child was telling the tale. One child's imagination led to the following pronouncement: "Your house is in the middle of the sea, so you can't go into it." This statement of "truth" provoked a long quarrel, culminating in shouting and tears.

Children intuitively know that even in pretend worlds there can only be one shared reality, one shared truth. And the one who defines that truth is a powerful person indeed. In our adult world of politics, culture, and knowledge, the dispute over who defines truth and reality is played out endlessly. Many people cynically conclude there is no truth, only power. Their final question becomes "*Whose* 'truth' will rule?" rather than "*What* is really true?" In this study we will see how we can trust God's Holy Spirit to lead us to the truth about God and about ourselves.

1. Is truth merely an issue of personal preference? In what areas of life is objective, absolute truth important?

READ JOHN 14:15-27.

2. What titles does Jesus use for the Holy Spirit?

What do these descriptions imply to you about the Spirit's work?

3. Why did Jesus say he would ask for *another* Counselor to be with them (verse 16)? Who was the first?

4. Who will know the Spirit of truth (verses 16-20)?

How do they know him?

---

5. Why do you think Jesus emphasizes that both his teaching and the Holy Spirit's teaching come from the Father (verses 24-26)?

Why would this be important for Jesus' disciples to know?

6. In verses 15, 21, 23-24, Jesus talks about the importance of obedience. How does each statement build on the preceding one?

7. Why might Jesus have interwoven this teaching about obedience with his teachings on the Spirit as a Spirit of truth?

READ JOHN 15:26-27.

8. Where does the Spirit come from, and what is his task?

✐ 9. What do you think is the difference between "testifying" about something and just giving an opinion?

Why can the Spirit testify about Jesus?

10. Do you know Jesus well enough to testify on his behalf, or can you only give an opinion about him? Elaborate.

READ JOHN 16:5-15.

11. What more do you learn about the Holy Spirit (verses 8-13)?

How would the Spirit's knowledge of truth relate to each of these different areas of the Spirit's work?

12. What is the Holy Spirit's ultimate purpose (verse 14)?

How does this add to what you observed in question 8?

13. Do you personally believe the Holy Spirit is the Spirit of truth? If so, how might that reality affect your life? If not, why not?

The Spirit of Wisdom

1 CORINTHIANS 1:17–2:5

When I was a child, I watched Superman on Saturday mornings. In spite of the silly melodrama and cardboard characters, there was something deeply satisfying about Superman's exploits on black and white TV. Good guys were always rescued in the nick of time. Slightly stupid bad guys faced prompt humiliation and the strong arm of the law.

At one point later in my life, I found myself quite angry at God. I was surprised how deeply the Superman myth corresponded with my expectations of how life *ought* to be. The gist of my complaint? In my wisdom, I wanted God to be like the "Man of Steel"—rescuing the innocent, dispatching the wicked, flying in to vindicate my faith. Instead, I saw the innocent suffer, the wicked often prosper, and my faith waver. Obviously, in God's wisdom, his solutions to our struggles are not like Superman's conquests. Why? What is the wisdom of God's way? Isaiah 11:2 tells us that God's Spirit is the "Spirit of wisdom." In this lesson we compare the Holy Spirit's wisdom to the wisdom of this world.

1. What kind of people does the world honor or recognize as wise? Why?

READ 1 CORINTHIANS 1:17-25.

2. What is the "message of the cross" Paul refers to in verse 18? (See John 3:16-18 for clarification.)

3. A "stumbling block" is an obstacle to belief. Why is the message of "Christ crucified" a stumbling block to the Jews and foolishness to the Greeks (verses 22-23)?

4. In what ways and for what reasons do you think the message of the cross is a similar obstacle to people today?

5. What are some of the differences between those who see the cross as foolishness and those who don't (verses 18, 21, 23-24)?

Which of these groups do you most identify with? Why?

6. Give some examples of what might be included in the "wisdom of this world" that Paul refers to in verses 20-21?

Why is the wisdom of the world not enough to find God's wisdom?

7. How would preaching about Christ with words of human wisdom empty the cross of its power?

READ 1 CORINTHIANS 1:26-31.

8. Paul goes on to contrast human wisdom with God's wisdom. Why does God choose to work through the weak things of this world rather than the strong (verses 27-29)?

9. What kind of wisdom has Christ become for us (verse 30)? How is this wisdom related to the "message of the cross"?

10. Trace through this passage and note how God's power and wisdom are related. Contrasting the world's wisdom with God's power, what is the irony of God's power?

READ 1 CORINTHIANS 2:1-5.

11. Paul resoundingly rejected men's wisdom in favor of God's. How did the Holy Spirit demonstrate the way God's wisdom works through Paul?

12. How does God's wisdom and power bring us to faith in Christ differently than human persuasion would? In what are we resting (verses 4-5)?

13. Read 1 Corinthians 1:25 again. When have you found it difficult to trust God's seeming "foolishness" and "weakness"?

How can a new understanding of the Spirit's wisdom give you a different perspective on your life? Ask God to help you accept, understand, and be empowered by his wisdom.

The Spirit of Revelation and Understanding

EPHESIANS 1:15-19; 1 CORINTHIANS 2:6-16

As slides of paintings flicked across the screen in my Renaissance and Baroque art history classes, I realized I had one advantage many of my fellow students lacked—a Sunday school background. Not that Sunday school prepared me to tell a Michelangelo from a Raphael, but I did know Abraham's story from Moses' from David's from Paul's. It's been said that a picture is worth a thousand words, but European religious art is largely incomprehensible to those who don't know the Bible accounts on which these sculpted and painted images are based. Each student could have speculated a different scenario without guessing who or what was really depicted or, even more important, what it meant. We could all "see," but not all of us could understand.

Whether they are on video or in a four-hundred-year-old painting, visual images alone have profound limitations when it comes to communicating meaning and understanding. For this, we need words and language. Watching God's activity in history would leave us puzzled if there were no words, no explanations. Part of his work has always been explaining himself—with language. His words come to us through the Bible and through the living Word, Jesus Christ. But behind all of these explanations lies his official "explainer": the Holy Spirit of revelation.

1. When have you seen an event and wondered what was happening? Would an explanation in words have made things clearer? Elaborate.

READ EPHESIANS 1:15-19.

2. Paul is writing here to the Christians in Ephesus. What does he specifically ask God to grant them (verse 17)? To what end?

3. What else does Paul pray for them?

4. Why do you think Paul asks God to teach them all these things instead of just explaining it to them himself?

5. What part does the Holy Spirit have to do with these requests by Paul?

Why is the Holy Spirit so essential for the fulfillment of these requests?

READ 1 CORINTHIANS 2:6-16.

6. How is God's wisdom described in verses 6-9?

7. What ways of discovering and knowing things are considered inadequate for understanding what "God has prepared for those who love him" (verse 9)?

8. Why do you think these human ways of knowing are insufficient?

9. Who automatically knows the secret thoughts of God (verses 10-11)? How?

10. According to verses 12-13, what things does the Spirit help a Christian do?

    Have you experienced this in your life? Discuss.

11. How does the person without God's Spirit react to God's revelation (verse 14)? Why?

⌕ 12. Why do you think there is such an emphasis on "words" in verse 13?

13. Ask the Holy Spirit to show you which areas in your life need a truer understanding of God. List them.

Then ask the Holy Spirit to reveal God's thoughts to you so that you may truly know him better.

The Spirit of Life

EXODUS 20:1-17; ROMANS 8:1-14

O n the advice of an established portrait painter, I bought a life-sized model of a skull to help me learn to draw the structure and planes of the human head. I've dubbed it "J.R." and my children have peered into its cranium and worked its jaw, divided between revulsion and curiosity. But even attaching a silly name to it did not take away the sense of fear and mystery that this universal symbol of death evokes.

Death is the ultimate spoiler of all we hold dear. We do not want to die, and we diligently flee awareness of death by pursuing life on our own terms. The Bible teaches that we have all inherited and participate in Adam's legacy of sin and death (Romans 5:12). Adam sinned by breaking one command. We have broken many. Adam died. We also die—after experiencing myriad smaller deaths of dreams, relationships, and purpose along the paths of our lives. What hope do we have in the face of this powerful enemy? Let's look at God's provision for us through his Spirit of life.

1. Why can't we just accept death as a natural part of life?

READ EXODUS 20:1-17.

2. What types of relationships are covered by the Ten Commandments?

3. *Sin* has been defined as "missing the mark." What happens to each relationship listed above when we "miss the mark" by not following God's commands?

4. Think about how physical death affects relationships. In what ways are the effects of *sin* on relationships similar?

READ ROMANS 8:1-14.

5. What different ways is the term "law" used—in the legal sense (like a society's civil or moral code), or as a description of the natural order of things (like the law of gravity), or both (verses 2-4)? Explain.

How are sin and death a law?

6. In contrast, what is the law of the Spirit of life (verses 1-4)?

How does this law affect our lives?

7. All people, even those who know nothing about God, hate the *consequences* of sin, but they continue to sin. Why is that (verses 5-8)?

8. What is God's remedy for our sinful thoughts and desires?

9. How does God redeem the ultimate consequences of sin—our spiritual death and our physical death (verses 9-11)?

10. In what ways does submitting to the control of the Spirit restore life (verses 12-14)?

    How do you think we can "put to death" the misdeeds of the sinful nature?

11. Look back over this passage and find all the ways in which the Holy Spirit is part of God's plan to give us life.

12. Are there any areas in your life where it seems that the law of death still reigns? How might you submit these areas to the Spirit of life?

The Spirit of Grace and Freedom

GALATIANS 2:15–3:5; 5:13-26

In grade school, getting off the lumbering, yellow school bus and walking up the driveway to my house was like slipping through a portal from one world to another. There was a sense of relief and release and sanctuary. No more anonymous rules designed to keep five hundred kids in check. No more striving for acceptance. I could leave my "public face" behind. It wasn't that there weren't rules at home, or that we were free to be our worst selves. But there was always a kind of freedom and grace at home that made it, well, home.

There are parallels to this in our relationship with God. The Holy Spirit is the Spirit of grace (Hebrews 10:29) and freedom. Let's look into Galatians and see what that means.

1. What place or places do you consider a sanctuary, or "home"? Why?

READ GALATIANS 2:15–3:5.

  ∂ 2.   Paul is obviously upset with the Galatians. Why?

  ∂ 3.   In 3:3, Paul refers to a goal. What is that goal (see 2:15-17)?

    4.   By what two means have the Galatians tried to obtain this goal? Compare and contrast these differing ways.

    5.   What can the Spirit do that the law cannot?

READ GALATIANS 5:13-26.

    6.   What kind of freedom does the Spirit give us (verses 13-14)? Are we free to do anything we wish? Explain.

7. List the acts of the sinful nature and the fruit of the Holy Spirit given in verses 19-23.

Acts of sinful nature   Fruit of the Spirit

8. What are some differences between an *act* and a *fruit*?

9. Why do you suppose the *acts* of the sinful nature are compared here to the *fruit* of the Spirit?

10. Both the Spirit and the law oppose sin. Why, then, can't we use both ways together to gain righteousness?

11. What does the list of fruit tell us about the nature of the Holy Spirit?

12. We all need a safe sanctuary in which to grow. How is the grace and freedom you have in Christ con-ducive to the growth of the fruit of the Spirit in your life? In what areas do you need to grow more?

The Spirit
of Adoption

JOHN 8:31-47; GALATIANS 3:26–4:7;
ROMANS 8:15-17

F athers occupy a special place in their children's hearts.
Working on a project with Dad is about the greatest
thing going for my three young children. One way children
know who they are is by knowing their dad. For good or for ill,
their father's name and character are part of their heritage. In
biblical times, this identity between father and children was
even more clearly seen. A father's land and trade would become
his children's. All the labor invested in their father's work would
eventually come back as part of the children's inheritance. In
contrast, a slave had no inheritance nor special privileges that
the natural son enjoyed. Although a son could fall into slavery
through economic or political circumstances, a slave's status
could only be changed through a redemptive exchange of some
kind. Even so, a slave-turned-freedman could never become a
"son"—and thus an heir—unless he was also adopted.

Because Christ has paid the redemptive price for us, it is
possible for us to become children of God through "the Spirit
of adoption" (Romans 8:15, KJV). We can become his sons and

daughters who share in an amazing inheritance. This study looks at the Holy Spirit's part in this special relationship.

1. What further similarities and contrasts can you think of between a father/child relationship and a slave/master relationship?

READ JOHN 8:31-47.

2. Jesus claims that his teachings will set people free. Why don't the Jews see themselves as needing to be "set free" (verse 33)?

3. What kind of slavery and freedom is Jesus talking about?

How does he compare slaves and sons?

4. Who do the Jews claim as their fathers?

How does Jesus counter their claims?

5. What characterizes true children of God (verses 31, 42, 47)?

6. According to the description in verses 44-47, what kind of "father" is the devil? How can he be expected to care for his "children"?

READ GALATIANS 3:26–4:7.

7. How are God's children different from each other? How are they the same (verses 26-28)?

8. By what means does God grant sonship to slaves?

9. What is the Holy Spirit's part in our adoption as children of God?

10. *Abba* is Aramaic for "Daddy." Who can call God by this title?

How does believing that you can come to God as "Daddy" modify your view of him?

READ ROMANS 8:15-17.

11. Describe what happens to a person who receives the Spirit of sonship. What bondages are broken? What privileges are granted?

12. Some Bible versions translate verse 15 as the "Spirit of adoption." What does the idea of being adopted add to the meaning of sonship?

13. How can we know that our sonship/adoption is real—by experience, by faith, by both?

In what ways have you experienced the affirmation of the Holy Spirit in your life?

The Spirit
of Prophecy

2 PETER 1:19-21; DEUTERONOMY 18:9-22;
13:1-4; 1 JOHN 4:1-6

Human beings have a frustratingly limited scope of knowledge. It is part of our nature to be intrigued by prophets who speak to us of unseen mysteries. In our fallen state, we are often both sitting ducks for phonies and offended by those who speak God's truth. Sometimes it seems easier to just ignore the whole topic. Yet the Bible is filled with accounts of God speaking through prophets. Loved, honored, vilified, or killed; whether their messages were embraced or rejected, prophets were never ignored.

But not all prophets are created equal. The Bible divides them into three kinds: charlatans who exercise their own imaginations, occult practitioners of sorcery and divination, and legitimate proclaimers of God's messages. True prophecy not only tells of things to come, but God also uses it to paint vivid portraits of himself. God's Spirit is the one who speaks God's message through human lips and pens. Let's look at the Holy Spirit as the Spirit of genuine prophecy.

1. Today, a mind-boggling array of holy men, gurus, ayatollahs, shaman, visionaries, and traditional healers call for our attention with claims of divine inspiration. Name a few.

READ 2 PETER 1:19-21.

2. What three "players" are involved in legitimate scriptural prophecy? What part does each one play?

3. In this passage, Peter is referring to the Old Testament prophets. Why would Christians do well to pay heed to these scriptures?

READ DEUTERONOMY 18:9-22.

4. These are God's instructions to the Israelites before they go into the promised land of Canaan. How did the nations in this area pursue supernatural knowledge and powers?

What is God's judgment on their methods? Why?

5. In contrast, how does God promise to instruct the Israelites?

6. According to verses 17-18, how will the prophet know what to say?

7. Why would the safeguards given in verses 20-22 distinguish the Holy Spirit's inspiration from other prophetic messages?

READ DEUTERONOMY 13:1-4.

8. What are some other measures by which to judge whether or not the Holy Spirit is speaking through prophets?

9. Thinking back to your answer for question 1, how do some of today's "prophets" measure up against this standard?

READ 1 JOHN 4:1-6.

10. What does John encourage the Christians here to do?

Why is this an important task for believers?

11. Can a prophesying spirit masquerade as the Holy Spirit? If so, how can such a counterfeit be exposed?

12. Can we expect the world to recognize the Spirit? Why or why not?

Where can we go to find hope in the midst of false teachers and evil in this world (verse 4)?

13. Do you need to renounce any illegitimate prophets or occult activities with which you may have been involved? Ask the Holy Spirit to help you discern his words and work from the many false claims of prophetic insight today.

The Spirit of Power

1 KINGS 19:7-18; EPHESIANS 3:14-21

It was a challenge between the prophets of Baal and the prophet of Yahweh: two altars, two bulls, two claims of sovereignty. "The god who answers by fire—he is God" (1 Kings 18:24). Four hundred and fifty parched prophets of Baal danced themselves into near exhaustion on Mount Carmel, but Baal's altar and sacrifice remained untouched. Elijah readied a second altar by saturating it with water. Then the solitary prophet petitioned Yahweh—the true God of Israel. Breathtaking fire crackled out of heaven and utterly consumed the sacrifice, the stones, the soil, and the water in the trench. "The LORD—he is God!"

What an awesome display of power! Yahweh had exposed the futility of the pagan order of things and demonstrated his moral character and strength. Sometimes we wistfully long to see God's power "really do something," like his explosive show of force on Mount Carmel. But while we are longing for the spectacular, we may be missing what he is, in fact, doing quietly in our lives day by day. Let's look at another way God's Spirit of power can work changes in our lives.

1. What sort of things do you equate with a show of God's power?

READ 1 KINGS 19:7-18.

2. Following the victory on Mount Carmel, Queen Jezebel responded with murderous threats against Elijah. The prophet flees for his life and hides in a cave, depressed and despairing. What is Elijah's complaint (verse 10)?

   How does God respond to it (verse 11)?

3. What was the sequence of events that occurred as Elijah waited for the Lord to pass by?

4. How was Elijah's experience of God's power different this time from the confrontation on Mount Carmel?

Which experience most strengthened and encouraged Elijah to persevere? Why?

5. In biblical terms, the *heart* or inner being is the hidden core of a person, while the outer person is the appearance presented to others. From what, with what, and through what, does God strengthen our inner beings (verses 16-17)?

6. According to verse 17, why do we need this strength?

How is this different from what we normally think we need strength for?

7. Note the three ways the Spirit's power is needed in our lives. In which of these areas do you most feel the need for God's strengthening right now?

8. Why is it so important to grow toward understanding the full scope of Christ's love?

9. Why do you think we need the Holy Spirit to fully grasp Christ's love?

10. Have you recognized God's hand and the Spirit's power when he has done something beyond your imagination or thinking? Explain.

11. How might these "silent" aspects of the Holy Spirit's power encourage you to trust God more?

12. Turn Ephesians 3:14-19 into a personal prayer for yourself and others you love.

The Spirit Who Leads

ISAIAH 63:11-14; ACTS 10:9-23;
13:1-5; 16:6-10

The small civilian plane with American citizens aboard had crashed in a remote, triple-canopy rain forest of Liberia. Seven highly trained U.S. Marines confidently volunteered for the search party. But it was a weather-beaten, barefoot Liberian who led them. He knew this rugged wilderness as home, while to the Americans it was alien territory, in spite of their sophisticated skills. And it was the African's sharp eyes that picked out a small piece of plastic from the plane in the undergrowth. Due to his unerring guidance, the search party avoided pitfalls and completed their mission.

Each of us is thrust at birth into a lifelong journey that is as unknown as an uncharted rain forest. Our paths are unique. No one can tell what twists and turns await us. God has given us general guidelines in his Word. Yet, even with these wilderness instructions firmly in hand, we still may lack the specific guidance and information needed to carry out our missions successfully. What are we to do? By looking at ways that God has led people in the Bible, we'll see God's provision for our own journeys through the Holy Spirit, our guide and companion.

1. Think of a time when a mentor, guide, or leader helped you accomplish something. Briefly tell your story.

READ ISAIAH 63:11-14.

⌀ 2. The prophet Isaiah reminds the people of Israel of God's work among them during their exodus from Egypt. Who was the divine agent and who was the human agent of God's leading here?

What was God's purpose in leading them (verses 12, 14)?

⌀ 3. Think about Moses' task of leading a million people through a hostile wilderness. Was the Spirit's guidance a mere nicety, or a necessity?

What might have happened without it?

READ ACTS 10:9-23.

4. What happened to Peter on the roof?

    How did Peter receive instructions in this case?

5. What was Peter doing before he was led so specifi-
    cally (verse 9)?

    Is there a connection between what he was doing
    and God's leading? Discuss.

6. What was God's ultimate purpose for this
    encounter? (See Acts 10:34-46.)

READ ACTS 13:1-5.

7. Who was gathered here? What were they doing?

8. How is this instance of guidance different from the previous accounts? How is it the same?

Read Acts 16:6-10.

9. How did the Spirit of Jesus (i.e., the Holy Spirit) lead Paul and his companions in regard to Asia and Bithynia?

How would you have felt, had you been in their company?

10. What additional things do you learn from this story about how the Spirit guides?

✐ 11. In each of these instances in Acts, what are some of the Holy Spirit's "ulterior motives" for leading people as he does?

How might these aims help us distinguish the Spirit's voice and leading from our own "voice" or thinking?

12. Think about some of the pluses and minuses of trying to live life under the guidance of the Spirit. How can some of the pitfalls be avoided?

13. How can you gain confidence in hearing and following the Spirit? Ask God to help you "hear" the Spirit's voice clearly, discern wisely, and obey readily.

The Spirit Who Anointed Jesus for Ministry

LUKE 3:21-23; 4:1-21, 38-44

In the Old Testament, expert perfumers compounded God's precious anointing oil according to his explicit instructions. The oil was God's for consecrating whomever he chose, and it represented the Holy Spirit. When God sent a messenger to pour costly oil over the head of a prophet, priest, or king, God demonstrated through the anointing ceremony that this person was chosen and set apart for a special purpose among God's people. He also simultaneously empowered the anointed one with the Holy Spirit for the assigned task.

Jesus Christ did not astound others with prophetic dreams and visions at an early age, nor was he of priestly lineage or born in a wealthy palace. Yet he is portrayed in the New Testament as a prophet, priest, and king. How did he come into his rightful, anointed position as Messiah and Lord? Let's look at the Holy Spirit's part in Jesus' ministry.

1. How do we confer power and authority on leaders today? What sort of people/positions still require such ceremonies?

READ LUKE 3:21-23.

2. How old was Jesus here? What happened when he was baptized?

⊘ 3. Who would have heard the voice from heaven?

Why do you think the Holy Spirit was made visible? What purpose might this have served?

READ LUKE 4:1-13.

⊘ 4. What happened to Jesus immediately after his baptism? Why is it significant that this happened *after* his baptism and not before?

⊅5. Why was it important that this confrontation with
Satan occurred *before* Jesus continued on in his
mission and ministry?

READ LUKE 4:14-21.

6. Following his time of temptation, what did Jesus
begin to do in Galilee?

⊅7. After reading the passage from Isaiah 61:1-2, what
bold claim did Jesus make in verse 21?

List the specific aspects of his claim noted in this
Old Testament prophecy that would mark his
ministry.

⊅8. How was Jesus anointed (verse 18)?

READ LUKE 4:38-44.

9. What remarkable things had Jesus been doing
    (verses 38-41)? What was his ultimate purpose
    (verses 42-44)?

10. Compare the works of Jesus listed in these verses
    with those described in the passage he quoted from
    Isaiah. Note the parallels.

11. Prior to Jesus' baptism, there is no record of miracles
    nor claims of authority made by Jesus. Why do you
    think this changed after his baptism?

12. If Jesus' ministry was so intertwined with the Holy
    Spirit, what does that tell us about our need for the
    Holy Spirit? Ask God to show you how to surrender
    more of your life to the Spirit's fullness.

The Spirit Who Empowers Us for Ministry

ACTS 1:1-11; 2:1-4, 36-39; 1 CORINTHIANS 12:4-11

I was not a natural athlete while growing up. I particularly hated junior high volleyball, where my more coordinated classmates despised and humiliated me. No matter how much I was scolded, exhorted, or commanded, no one could give me that innate ability to play well and contribute positively to the team. It was with relief that I finally said good-bye to my last required physical education class. Later in college, I joined some "for-fun" volleyball games. To my amazement, I discovered I had become an asset to my team instead of a liability. Although the change was probably a matter of maturity and confidence, I felt like I had been inexplicably gifted with coordination and grace. I certainly had not attained it through my own effort or force of will.

Spiritually speaking, it is as absurd to command Christians to carry out God's work on their own as it was for my friends to shout at me to improve my athletic abilities. There are some things we simply can't do on our own. But God himself has provided a way for us to be graced with the ability to fulfill the tasks he has for each of us. He does it through his Spirit who empowers us for ministry.

1. Have you ever wanted to be a part of a team or group project but felt you had nothing to contribute? How did you feel?

READ ACTS 1:1-11.

2. For what gift are the disciples to wait?

What will happen when they receive this gift?

3. This particular command and promise from Jesus is sandwiched between his death and resurrection and his ascension to heaven. What might be some advantages of the indwelling of the Holy Spirit over Jesus' physical presence among his disciples?

READ ACTS 2:1-4.

4. What are the two striking images used to describe the Spirit's entrance?

   What do these images reveal about the Spirit and his kind of empowerment?

5. How did the Spirit empower the apostles to begin to fulfill the words of Jesus in Acts 1:8?

   How was this gift a powerful symbol of God's intention for the gospel?

READ ACTS 2:36-39.

6. The apostle Peter is boldly addressing the crowd in Jerusalem. According to his words, who can receive the Holy Spirit? How?

7. Why do you think your sins need to be forgiven before you can be indwelt by the Holy Spirit?

READ 1 CORINTHIANS 12:4-11.

8. What are the different ways the Holy Spirit provides for our common good as God's people together (verses 4-7)?

9. According to verses 7 and 11, if a person is indwelt by the Holy Spirit, will he or she automatically be given a way to contribute to the body of Christ? Explain.

10. The word *manifest* means "to be made clear or evident." List the ways the Spirit is manifested in different individuals.

11. What clues does this list of the Spirit's manifestations and gifts give us about what the Holy Spirit is like?

12. Pick one gift and explain why it is important to the body of Christ.

13. How has the Holy Spirit empowered you for service to others? Ask God to help you understand your own and others' gifts better, and to help you effectively manifest his Spirit.

The Spirit of Unity

1 CORINTHIANS 12:12-13, 21-27;
EPHESIANS 4:1-16

I 've always been partial to professional football teams' brilliantly hued uniforms. The navy and orange team colors of the Chicago Bears are my favorite. But under those matching helmets and jerseys is a full range of ethnic backgrounds, histories, and temperaments. No player cancels out his individual distinctives to become a Bear. But when the game begins, one thing takes precedence—the team colors. Yet, even though each Bear wears the same colors, the players are not interchangeable. Swap a quick, slender running back for a lineman the size of a home appliance and the results are disastrous. Everyone must play his own position. No player can come out and be "the Bears" alone.

Teamwork helps win games, but a colorful team jersey easily slips on and off. Unity among Christians can break down just as easily. What is strong enough and great enough to pull Christ's people together, across time and language and cultures? Let's see how God deals with unity amidst diversity among first-century Christians in the cosmopolitan cities of Corinth and Ephesus.

1. Think of a group to which you belong. What unites these people so they function as a group?

READ 1 CORINTHIANS 12:12-13, 21-27.

2. Note the types of people listed in verse 13. Why might they not naturally choose to rub shoulders with each other?

3. In these verses, what does the analogy of the body represent?

   Who or what holds these diverse people together as a body (verses 12-13)?

4. What is God's desire for his body (verses 24-26)?

READ EPHESIANS 4:1-16.

5. Whose unity are Christians to keep (verse 3)?

Why doesn't it say "your unity"?

6. Think of the metaphor in verse 4 of "one body and one Spirit." How are human spirits and bodies interdependent? What happens to a body without a spirit? A spirit without a body?

7. Recall your answer to question 1. Compare human kinds of unity with the unity in the Spirit. How are they the same? How are they different?

8. What is the purpose of the gifts listed in verses 11-13?

How is this goal characteristic of the Holy Spirit's work?

9. What kind of things war against unity in the body (verse 14)?

10. Why do you think the process of unity and attaining maturity in Christ described in verses 12-16 is dependent on the proper outworking of the Spirit's gifts?

✐ 11. Given this discussion on unity, why is it so important that Christians discover and use their spiritual gifts? Explain.

12. If you are part of the body of Christ, do you find joy in using your gifts in the body? How can you help build unity and maturity in the church?

13. Conclude this study by meditating on what you have learned about the Holy Spirit's person, character, and work. Ask God to help you submit more fully to him so that he, through the Spirit of his Son, is expressed more richly and deeply in you.

Leader's Notes

Study 1: The Spirit of Truth

Question 3. Isaiah 9:6 prophesies that Jesus will be the "Wonderful Counselor." See also John 16:7.

Question 5. God is clearly the expert authority when it comes to the truth about everything. As Creator and sustainer of the world, he has total knowledge of all that is. When Jesus links his and the Holy Spirit's teaching to God, he claims the same ultimate authority of absolute truth for their teaching. He also indirectly claims that both he and the Holy Spirit are one with God.

Question 6. If you love, you will obey. If you love and obey, then the Father and Jesus will love you. If you love and obey and the Father loves you, *we* (meaning the Father and Son through the Holy Spirit) will come to you. This is an example of the mysterious covenantal relationship God has set up between himself and us human beings. He asks an obedience of faith based on love, not law.

Question 7. Obedience to God is an act of faith. By obeying, we say that we believe the truth and reality of his kingdom is more real than the world we see every day. When we are obedient to God, his truth rules in our lives.

Question 9. To testify is to affirm what you know to be true by firsthand knowledge, either as a witness to an event or as an expert on a subject through research and study (see 1 John 1:1-3). An opinion includes a large part of interpretation and speculation and may or may not be true. The Holy Spirit can testify firsthand about Jesus because of the eternal relationship between the Father, the Son, and the Spirit.

STUDY 2: THE SPIRIT OF WISDOM

Question 2. In 1 Corinthians 1:10-17, Paul warns the Corinthians against the natural tendency to trust in and identify with human leaders more than they do Jesus. Paul reminds them that the central message of the cross is Christ crucified (1 Corinthians 1:23). Jesus won salvation for us through the apparent "weakness" of submitting himself to suffering and death on the cross.

Question 4. There are many reasons Christ's death on the cross remains an obstacle to people. One reason is that it confronts us with our sin—an unfashionable and uncomfortable concept. Another is that the remedy God requires for these sins— Jesus' crucifixion—seems so bloody, brutal, and "unmodern." Urge the group to come up with other reasons the cross may look foolish to an unbeliever.

Question 7. When the gospel is preached through human wisdom, we are often manipulated by the preacher appealing to our wants, desires, and fears, without confronting our genuine guilt and need for repentance from sin. Only the Holy Spirit can persuade willful people to make this step of submission to the cross.

Question 10. The world seeks power in order to control and find success and fulfillment. Christ revealed the wisdom of God by submitting to the power of the world, allowing people to kill him. Through this act, the greater power of God was demonstrated by turning this seeming defeat to a final redemptive victory.

STUDY 3: THE SPIRIT OF REVELATION AND UNDERSTANDING

Question 7. Human observation (seeing), the accumulation of human teaching (hearing), and human imagination/reasoning (conceiving), are not enough to usher us into the mind of God and his plans for us.

Question 8. Human ways of understanding and knowing God's ways are insufficient because God's kingdom and ways are foreign and contrary to a fallen and rebellious humanity. His plans and purposes for us are part of a larger reality which is too great for human minds alone to unravel. We can only know in so far as God's Spirit reveals his thoughts.

Question 12. God's relationship to people is played out in history, and the core of history is "story." Stories require some form of language. The "Who? What? When? and Where?" might be conveyed without specific words, but words are needed for understanding and explaining the "Why?" of a story, and "What does it mean?" For example, if we don't know the *why* of Jesus' death, then his death is no more than just another criminal execution. The symbol of the cross would be meaningless.

STUDY 4: THE SPIRIT OF LIFE

Question 2. The Ten Commandments outline the proper order of relationship to God (Exodus 20:3-7); to the created order (verses 4-5); to work and rest (verses 8-11); to family (verse 12); to spouse and community (verses 13-17). Jesus summed up all of the relationships covered in the Law when he said, "Love the Lord your God with all your heart and with all your soul and with all your mind and with all your strength" and "Love your neighbor as yourself" (Mark 12:30-31).

Question 4. Death's central characteristic is separation—the untimely severing of important connections. Sins are selfish and unfaithful acts and attitudes that likewise divide and destroy relationships. Sin (breaking faith) separates us from God, from each other, ultimately even from ourselves.

Question 5. In these verses the word *law* is really used in two ways: as a description of the natural order of things (Romans 8:1-2), and in the legal sense, as God's revealed law (verses 3-4). The "law of sin and death" appears to show a principle of natural consequences. Romans 6:23 tells us "the wages of sin is death, but the gift of God is eternal life in Christ Jesus our Lord." Death follows sin as naturally as falling will follow jumping from an airplane. The law of gravity doesn't *cause* falling; it simply describes what happens. Likewise, the law of death describes the aftermath of sin. Death is an inevitable consequence of sin without God's direct intervention.

Question 6. Righteousness begets life as a natural consequence. Since we cannot attain righteousness on our own, we are cut off from God, the source of life. In Christ, the requirements for righteousness are met. Through him, we enter into the law of the Spirit of life, and new life follows. While sin and death sever connections, the Spirit of life brings reconciliation and reconnection.

STUDY 5: THE SPIRIT OF GRACE AND FREEDOM

Question 2. The early Christians were largely Jewish converts. There was much debate over what parts of the old Jewish law were still to be obeyed. Paul writes against this legalism and reproves the Galatian Christians for allowing themselves to be convinced that following the law was still necessary for salvation (see Galatians 1:1–2:14). He reminds them that life in the Spirit is not based on following rules, but based on a relationship with God through the Holy Spirit.

Question 3. Their goal was justification—a right standing—before God. Likewise, most of us want to be confident that we are free from guilt and blame and thus righteous. But we cannot accomplish this on our own.

Question 8. Fruit comes when a plant is nourished and the time is right. This fruit is naturally determined by the plant's genetic makeup (apples do not grow on grapevines). Fruit also benefits others. Our spiritual fruit will flow naturally out of our life in the Spirit. On the other hand, to do *acts* implies volition. Our purposes and choices are carried out through our actions. The sinful nature acts to satisfy itself and benefits no one. Even a "religious nature"—one which tries to keep the law—ultimately acts to satisfy itself rather than benefit others.

Question 10. The law can define righteousness and condemn sin, but the sin nature still lives and drives us, even when we know, through the law, that our sin is wrong. Through Christ the sin nature is crucified (Galatians 2:21). Through the Spirit, that nature's desires are being replaced by godly desires. Trusting Christ's work acknowledges our inability to be righteous. Trusting in righteous works for salvation goes back to hoping that we have the ability to either be sinless or to pay for sins on our own.

STUDY 6: THE SPIRIT OF ADOPTION

Question 4. The Jews first claim Abraham as father, then they claim God alone. Jesus counters by contrasting their murderous intentions with Abraham's deeds of faith. If they were really children of God, they would believe what Jesus taught. Jesus then names the devil, with his rejection of truth, as their true father.

Question 7. All who have faith in Jesus as the Christ, or Messiah/Savior, are children of God. They are all one in Christ and part of an adopted family greater than any of our human or ethnic distinctions. However, those who have not been redeemed are not sons, but slaves to sin, and outside of God's family.

Question 8. In the pagan culture prevalent in Galatia, slaves were not freed outright. There had to be a payment of some kind of ransom. Sometimes the owners themselves arranged for a particular slave's redemption, so that a slave became a free man. But redeeming a slave was not the same as adopting him. Using this analogy, Paul explains that God ransoms us, who were slaves of sin, with his Son's death. Those who identify themselves with Christ and his shed blood are then redeemed and filled with the Son's Spirit, thus becoming adopted as children of God. We are redeemed and freed and adopted as sons and daughters.

Question 13. Sometimes Christians feel lost, abandoned, or disowned by God. When we don't *feel* connected, we doubt that we really belong. God's Spirit testifies as an expert witness that we belong to him anyway. Believing this as an act of faith can free us from our fears and eventually change our sense of alienation from God as well.

STUDY 7: THE SPIRIT OF PROPHECY

Question 3. A full range of God's character is revealed in Old Testament prophecy—from his tender mercy to his terrifying judgment. Prophetic writings can transform our limited perspectives on life by revealing God's sovereignty as he interacts with the human race from the distant past through the end of time. It is reassuring to know that our current troubles are part of a greater, overarching plan of redemption. Nothing we experience is arbitrary or capricious.

Question 4. The Canaanite peoples engaged in a variety of pagan/occult activities (Deuteronomy 18:10-15). These occult practices resulted in the loss of their homeland under God's judgment. When God had promised this land to Abraham over four hundred years earlier, God had foreseen the unrepentant attitudes of these Canaanite peoples and foretold their judgment (Genesis 15:12-16).

God hates occult practices because they are a perverse and

deceptive substitute for the real help people need—a right relationship with God. Occultism is the equivalent of throwing a
drowning man a concrete block.

Question 8. Even total accuracy does not legitimize a prophet
if the prophet uses his power to call people away from God.
The Holy Spirit would never inspire people to turn from God
(and thus from himself) toward some new god inconsistent
with what the Holy Spirit has already revealed.

STUDY 8: THE SPIRIT OF POWER

Question 6. We need power outside of ourselves for salvation.
Ever since Adam and Eve sinned in the Garden of Eden, the
human race has been spiritually dead. No matter how many
things we have tried on our own, we have not been able to
reestablish that original personal connection to God because we
have no power to grant ourselves spiritual life. Through Christ
our inner being is spiritually revived and the indwelling Holy
Spirit strengthens our newly resurrected spiritual nature, freely
giving us the faith we need to be able to trust and know God.

In addition, we usually think of needing strength to face
difficulties. But this implies that we also need strengthening to
receive and grasp all the good things we have in Christ.

Question 9. Given the experience most of us have with life,
without the direct intervention of the Holy Spirit we won't
naturally believe God loves us this completely. Believing that
God is good and loving is often an act of faith, and the Holy
Spirit is the one who empowers us to have this faith. See Ephesians 2:8-9.

STUDY 9: THE SPIRIT WHO LEADS

Question 2. See Exodus 12–16 for more specific details of how God led the Israelites out of Egypt.

Question 3. The Israelites had not been this way before and had no maps. It was desert country, barren and waterless. Without God's specific leading and miracles, this enormous group of people probably would have been killed by the pursuing Egyptians or died from exposure or starvation.

Question 6. The Spirit was leading the church to take the gospel to the Gentiles. Christ had intended that his offer of salvation would include the Gentiles, fulfilling the prophecy in Isaiah 49:6. Through Peter, the Spirit gave the Jewish believers direction and extra prodding to move into this uncharted territory.

Question 11. Each time the Spirit led God's people, they were seeking his help and were already involved in the process of obeying Christ by being his witnesses. Their testimony of Christ ultimately brought glory to God. (See John 17:1-5.) The Holy Spirit will never lead us in ways that dishonor God or his written Word. Nor will the Spirit's leading merely serve only our selfish ends and pride.

STUDY 10: THE SPIRIT WHO ANOINTED JESUS FOR MINISTRY

Question 3. God claimed Jesus as his Son before "all the people" who were there to hear John the Baptist. There had been neither prophets nor any visible mighty works of God for centuries before John came on the scene. In the midst of this crowd, God consecrated Jesus by the Holy Spirit for Jesus' special ministry. The voice and dove were part of a public pronouncement of God's intention to move again among his people in this generation. Even more so, it was a tangible sign that Jesus was blessed and chosen by God.

Question 4. Jesus was led by the Spirit into the wilderness and tempted by Satan. Since Jesus had been officially commissioned by God the Father through his baptism, he was an obvious target for Satan. Also, Jesus was specially equipped and anointed by the fullness of the Spirit to overcome this attack. Jesus had two natures—human and divine. His human nature needed the Holy Spirit's power as much as we do.

Question 5. God often tests and proves us before he allows us to come fully into our own calling. He made no special exception for Jesus, who was "tempted in every way, just as we are—yet was without sin" (Hebrews 4:15). Withstanding the kinds of temptations that have historically destroyed God's people was Christ's first step toward qualifying himself as the sinless one who could be the perfect, once-for-all sacrifice for sin, and one who could relate to our experiences.

Question 7. Jesus claims this Old Testament scripture applies to himself. All the Jews knew this to be a prophecy of the coming Messiah, or *Christ,* which means "the anointed One." Through these verses, Jesus sets up a standard by which his anointing and ministry can be measured, ultimately proving that he was the Christ, their Messiah.

Question 8. Human priests anointed people at God's command. As they were anointed, the Holy Spirit came upon them and empowered them to fulfill their task. God himself sent the Spirit in visible form to Jesus, anointing and empowering him for his mission.

STUDY 11: THE SPIRIT WHO EMPOWERS US FOR MINISTRY

Question 3. Jesus could spend time with only a limited number of people when he was on earth. The Holy Spirit does what Jesus did, except there is no limit to the number of people who can enjoy his intimate, daily fellowship.

Question 5. Rather than getting entangled in divisive controversy about speaking in tongues, direct the group to consider how the preaching of the gospel in all these languages to an incredibly diverse group of people foreshadows God's intention that his Word go to all the ends of the earth.

Question 7. God, through his Spirit, is not going to cohabit with another god and master—sin. God requires our exclusive allegiance. We do not have to be perfect and sinless to be indwelt, but sin's authority and rule must be broken through Christ. See Romans 6:23 and 8:1-11.

Question 9. Each Christian has been given a way by the Spirit to minister to other Christians in the corporate church. No one is left empty-handed. However, these gifts of the Spirit often need to be developed as the Christian matures.

Question 11. Note how many gifts parallel the Holy Spirit's nature and work which we have studied in this series. Each gift is actually an expression of one of his characteristics.

Study 12: The Spirit of Unity

Question 5. We are to keep the unity of the Spirit. As the Spirit indwells individual Christians, it is his unity as a person that binds us together. He can't be disunited from himself, regardless of whether or not we are getting along with each other. No commonality we can find as humans is ultimately enough to withstand our differences and sin. We need the supernatural help of the Spirit.

Question 6. A body without a spirit is dead. A human spirit cannot do or express anything without some kind of body. A spirit and body fit each other with a one-to-one correspondence. Likewise, Christ's body, his church, is ultimately one, with one Spirit giving life to his one body.

Question 7. Human unity is judged by superficial appearances of conformity. But often there are deep divisions under that common focus. The Spirit's unity is a deep, profound unity that often appears diverse or fractured. Going beyond superficial differences should bring God's people closer together, while moving past initial similarities often fragments human unity.

Question 11. In our last lesson we learned that the gifts were manifestations of the Spirit. Together, all of these different manifestations are like facets on a diamond—expressions of a greater whole. If some of the gifts are either withheld or disallowed, then pieces will be missing from the fullness of Christ in his body. Encourage the group to think and pray about how the Holy Spirit has gifted them and can use them in their local congregation of believers.

The Fisherman Bible Studyguide Series—
Get Hooked on Studying God's Word

Old Testament Studies

Genesis

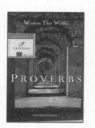

Proverbs

New Testament Studies

Mark

John

Acts 1-12

Acts 13-28

Romans

Philippians

Colossians

James

1, 2, 3 John

Revelation

Women of the Word

*Becoming Women
of Purpose*

*Wisdom for
Today's Woman*

Women Like Us

*Women Who
Believed God*

For more information, visit our Web site: www.waterbrookmultnomah.com

Topical Studies

Building Your House on the Lord

Discipleship

Encouraging Others

The Fruit of the Spirit

Growing Through Life's Challenges

Guidance and God's Will

Higher Ground

Lifestyle Priorities

The Parables of Jesus

Parenting with Purpose and Grace

Prayer

Proverbs & Parables

The Sermon on the Mount

Speaking Wisely

Spiritual Disciplines

Spiritual Gifts

Spiritual Warfare

The Ten Commandments

When Faith Is All You Have

Who Is the Holy Spirit?